DATE DUE	

NORTH CAROLINA

in words and pictures

BY DENNIS B. FRADIN

ILLUSTRATIONS BY RICHARD WAHL

MAPS BY LEN W. MEENTS

CHILDRENS PRESS ™

CHICAGO

3982

Trees cover more than 60 percent of North Carolina.

Library of Congress Cataloging in Publication Data

Fradin, Dennis B.
    North Carolina in words and pictures.

    SUMMARY: A brief history of the Tar Heel State with
a description of its countryside and major cities.
    1. North Carolina—Juvenile literature.
|1. North Carolina| I. Wahl, Richard, 1939-
II. Meents, Len W.   III. Title.
F254.5.F7   975.6   79-25291
ISBN 0-516-03933-4

Picture Acknowledgments:

UNITED STATES DEPARTMENT OF THE INTERIOR (USDI), NATIONAL PARK SERVICE (NPS), FORT RALEIGH NATIONAL HISTORIC SITE— Cover, pages 9, 10 (left), 11

USDI, NPS, CAPE HATTERAS NATIONAL SEASHORE—pages 15, 27, 30, 31, 42

USDI, NPS, CAPE LOOKOUT NATIONAL SEASHORE, BRUCE E. WEBER—page 29

USDI, NPS, BLUE RIDGE PARKWAY—page 2

NORTH CAROLINA MUSEUM OF HISTORY, STATE DEPARTMENT OF CULTURAL RESOURCES—pages 6, 10 (right)

USDI, NPS, MOORES CREEK NATIONAL MILITARY PARK—pages 17, 18

ARCHITECT OF THE U.S. CAPITOL—page 20

NORTH CAROLINA DEPARTMENT OF NATURAL AND ECONOMIC RESOURCES—pages 23, 34, 39

USDI, NPS, WRIGHT BROTHERS NATIONAL MEMORIAL, PHOTOS COURTESY OF THE LIBRARY OF CONGRESS—page 24

UNIVERSITY OF NORTH CAROLINA AT CHAPEL HILL—page 26

USS *NORTH CAROLINA* BATTLESHIP COMMISSION—page 28

TYRON PALACE COMMISSION, NEW BERN, NORTH CAROLINA—page 32

GREATER WINSTON-SALEM CHAMBER OF COMMERCE—pages 36, 37, 40

COVER—Thomas Hariot Natural Trail Toward Sound Overlook

North Carolina (care • oh • LYE • nah) is a mixture of old and new. Some mountain families live much as people lived a very long time ago. In the cities, modern factories turn out many products for all of America.

North Carolina is one of our most beautiful states. Trees cover more than 60 percent of the state. Bear and deer still live in the forests. In the spring, wild flowers fill the land with color. The state has much more . . .

Do you know which is the leading furniture-making state?

Do you know which is the leading tobacco-growing state?

Do you know where the Wright Brothers first flew their airplane?

Do you know where Virginia Dare—the first English child born in America—lived?

As you will learn, the answer to all these questions is the Tar Heel State—North Carolina!

The Appalachian (app • uh • LAY • chun) Mountains in North Carolina are the oldest mountains in the United States. They were folded out of the earth more than 200 million years ago. Grandfather Mountain in North Carolina is sometimes called *the* oldest mountain in the country.

From time to time, the land that is now North Carolina was under water. Fossils of sea life have been found in places that are now dry land. Sharks' teeth and whale bones have been found by North Carolina farmers.

The inland ocean dried. Trees and plants took root in the rich soil. Many kinds of animals came to live on the land. Mastodons (MASS • tuh • donz) and woolly mammoths (MAM • uths) roamed the land. They looked like big, hairy elephants. They all died out long ago. Deer and bear came to the forests, too.

The first people arrived more than 10,000 years ago. They roamed the countryside. They hunted bear and deer for food. Later they learned to grow corn and other crops. Those who farmed could settle in villages. Some of these ancient people buried their dead in large mounds. One such mound is at Town Creek.

These early people may have been related to the Indians who came later. At least 30 tribes lived in North Carolina. As many as 35,000 Indians may have

Artist John White's paintings of an Indian warrior (left) and an Indian chief below)

lived there. The Cherokee (CHAIR • uh • kee) were the biggest tribe. Other main tribes were the Tuscarora (tuss • kuh • ROAR • uh), Hatteras (HAT • er • uss), Catawba (kah • TAW • bah) and Chowanoc (cho • WAH • nuk).

Some Indians lived in long houses made of tree bark. Others lived in tents, called *tepees*. Many houses or tepees made a village.

Most of the Indians in North Carolina farmed. They grew corn, potatoes, squash, peas, and melons. They were also the first tobacco-growers in North Carolina. They smoked tobacco in stone pipes.

Indians also hunted deer and bear. They used bows and arrows or spears. They ate the meat. The skins were used to make clothes. Indians who lived near rivers built wooden dugout canoes. Then they fished in Carolina waters.

Near the coast, Indians collected clam shells. They used these shells for money. They called it *wampum*.

The Indians loved to tell stories, sing, and hold big feasts. The Cherokees held the Green Corn Dance at harvest time. The Indians loved sports, too.

Many unknown explorers may have seen the North Carolina coast. The first one we know about was an Italian. His name was Giovanni da Verrazano (jo • VAH • nee dah vair • uh • TZAH • no). He sailed for the king of France. Verrazano arrived in 1524. He explored the area of Cape Fear. He was impressed by the beauty of the area.

Spanish explorers came, too. They wanted gold. In about 1526 the Spanish explorer Lucas Vásquez de Ayllón (LOO • kuss VASS • cayth deh eye • lee • OHN) came. He formed a settlement near Cape Fear. It didn't last long. In 1540 the Spanish explorer Hernando De Soto (her • NAN • doh deh SO • toe) crossed the mountains in southwestern North Carolina. De Soto wanted gold. In fact, much gold was later found in North Carolina. But De Soto didn't find it. He didn't stay.

Earthworks of Fort Raleigh, the first colonists' fort

The English were the first to settle permanently in North Carolina. In 1584 Englishman Sir Walter Raleigh (RAW • lee) sent explorers to America. They were at sea for two months. Then they landed on Roanoke (ROE • uh • noke) Island in North Carolina. This was about July 4, 1585. The Indians were "most gentle," wrote Captain Arthur Barlowe.

The explorers took two Indians back with them to England. They told Raleigh about the beautiful land. The queen of England wanted him to start a colony. Raleigh sent out seven ships. They held more than a hundred settlers. In 1585 these settlers built Fort Raleigh on Roanoke Island.

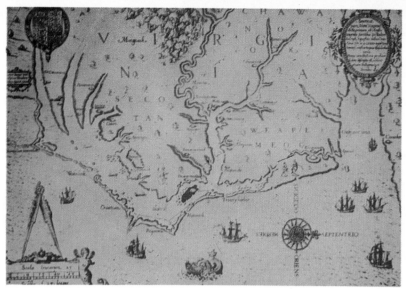

Above: An early John White map of the area
Right: A 1585 John White picture of an Indian village

This was the first English colony in what is now the United States. These settlers stayed for nearly a year. But they did not have enough food or supplies. They returned to England. One settler, John White, painted 75 pictures of Indians, plants, fish, birds, and other things. These pictures can still be seen in museums.

Raleigh sent a second group. This one was headed by John White. In July of 1587 the settlers reached Roanoke Island. The next month, on August 18, 1587, one of the best-known events in American history took place. John White's daughter, Eleanor White Dare, gave birth to a baby girl. The child was named Virginia Dare. Virginia Dare was the first English child born in what is now the United States.

The settlers built houses. But it was too late in the summer to grow crops. The people knew that they might starve. John White went back to England to get supplies. Because England was at war, he couldn't return to Roanoke Island until 1590. He found no people there. The fort and the houses were falling apart. The fate of these settlers is still a mystery. They are called the "Lost Colony."

John White paintings of a land crab and an Indian

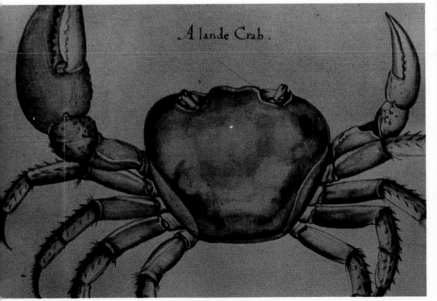

In 1607 England built its first permanent colony in America. This was at Jamestown, Virginia. In 1629 Charles I was king of England. He gave a large piece of land to Sir Robert Heath. The land was named *Carolana,* or *Carolina,* to honor King Charles I. It included all of present-day North Carolina and South Carolina, plus much other land.

Some Virginia people wanted a place that was less crowded. They went to what is now North Carolina. They bought land from the Indians. They became the first outsiders to settle permanently in North Carolina. The settlers built wooden houses. They had learned to grow corn from the Indians in Virginia. They also grew peas, beans, and tobacco.

In 1663 King Charles II gave some land to eight important men. These men were nobles who had helped the king. The land was the same land that had been given to Heath. The name Carolina was kept to honor King Charles II. The eight men were called *Lords Proprietors*. They appointed a governor. They sent more colonists to Carolina.

In 1677 some Carolina colonists became unhappy with their governor. They thought he was doing a bad job. They revolted. John Culpepper, their leader, became governor. The colonists governed their country for more than a year. The revolt is known as *Culpepper's Rebellion*.

In 1706 North Carolina's first town—Bath—was founded. In 1710 some English, German, and Swiss settlers founded New Bern. In 1712 Carolina was divided into North Carolina and South Carolina. Their governors were appointed by the Lords Proprietors.

More and more settlers poured into North Carolina. The Indians were losing their lands. They were angry. In 1711 the Tuscarora Indians went to war with the settlers. During the Tuscarora War, nearly the whole colony of North Carolina was wiped out. Finally, an army from South Carolina helped defeat the Indians at Fort Nohoroco on March 25, 1713. About 800 Indians were killed or captured. Many of the remaining Tuscarora went to live in New York. Their ancestors had lived there before moving south.

The settlers had other problems. In the early 1700s pirates preyed on ships that went in and out of both North Carolina and South Carolina. One of the most famous pirates was named Edward Teach. He was called Blackbeard. He carried a sword and pistols in his belt. Blackbeard hid his ship behind sand bars. When he saw a passing ship he attacked it and stole its goods. Finally, the English ship H.M.S. *Pearl* was sent to capture Blackbeard. Lieutenant Robert Maynard and Blackbeard

The pirate Blackbeard (Edward Teach)

met face to face near Ocracoke (OH • kruh • coke) Inlet.
Maynard and Blackbeard fired their pistols at the same
time. Blackbeard was hit. But he kept fighting. Finally,
one of Maynard's men killed Blackbeard with his sword.
It had taken 25 wounds to kill Blackbeard.

Another pirate who lurked on the Carolina coast was
Stede Bonnet. Anne Bonney was a famous woman pirate.
She dressed in men's clothes. She robbed ships, too.
Many of the pirates in the North Carolina area were
caught and hanged.

Finally, North Carolina was safe from pirates and Indian wars. Then more and more settlers arrived. In 1729 North Carolina became a royal colony. English, Scots-Irish, Scottish, and German people arrived. By 1765 there were about 120,000 settlers in North Carolina. Most farmed, but some fished or raised livestock. Some produced naval stores. Towns such as Wilmington (WILL • ming • tun), Hillsborough (HILLZ • burro), and Charlotte (SHAR • lut) were built. Some settlers moved closer and closer to the mountains.

North Carolinians had built their farms and towns themselves. They had fought pirates and Indians. During the 1760s, England heavily taxed the American colonies. This angered the people. "Give me liberty or give me death!" said Patrick Henry of Virginia. Many people in the colonies felt the same way. They decided to form a new country—the United States of America.

The American colonies went to war with England on April 19, 1776. This was called the Revolutionary War (rev • oh • LOO • shun • airy wore). More than 7,500 North Carolinians fought in George Washington's army. The first battle fought in North Carolina was at Moores Creek Bridge, near Wilmington, on February 27, 1776. American soldiers won this battle. That helped keep the English from capturing much of the South early in the war.

Below: Moores Creek, along the causeway
Right: A 2 pounder (cannon) of the type used at the Battle of Moores Creek Bridge

Above: Bicentennial recreation of a Minuteman and camp
Right: The Patriot Monument honors John Grady. He was the only Patriot to die as a result of the Battle of Moores Creek.

North Carolina men fought in big battles at Kings Mountain and Cowpens in South Carolina. They fought in many other places. On March 15, 1781 English forces met American forces at Guilford (GILL • ferd) Courthouse. That is near what is now Greensboro (GREENZ • burro). The English lost many men in this important battle. Soon afterward the English were driven from the Carolinas and Georgia.

The Americans won the Revolutionary War by 1783. A new country had been born—the United States of America. North Carolina became the twelfth state on November 21, 1789. In 1792 Raleigh was named the capital of the new state. It was a town laid out in the wilderness. Tar—from pine trees—was made in large amounts in North Carolina. North Carolina was nicknamed the *Tar Heel State*. No one knows exactly why. Some say it was because Revolutionary War soldiers once poured tar into a river to stop the English. Others say North Carolinians were called Tar Heels because they stuck to their posts during battles—as if tar were holding them down.

Today, North Carolinians are proud to be called Tar Heels. But after the Revolutionary War North Carolina had a nickname its people disliked. The state was called the *Rip Van Winkle* State. Rip Van Winkle was supposed to have slept for 20 years. North Carolina was "sleeping" in many ways. It had very few schools. Roads were poor. Even though the ocean was nearby, there were few good seaports. The cities weren't growing. In fact, more people were leaving North Carolina than going there.

Andrew Jackson portrait by Thomas Sully   James Knox Polk portrait by G.P.A. Healy

Two presidents—James Polk and Andrew Johnson—
were born in North Carolina. North Carolina and South
Carolina both claim to be the birthplace of President
Andrew Jackson. All three future presidents left North
Carolina. They went across the mountains to Tennessee.

One group was forced out of North Carolina by the
United States government. From 1838 to 1839 thousands
of Cherokee Indians in the southeastern United States

were taken from their homes. They were made to march all the way to Oklahoma. Many died on the way. They called this forced march the *Trail of Tears*. Some Cherokees escaped into the Great Smoky Mountains in North Carolina. Cherokee Indians still live there today.

North Carolina began to wake up in the 1830s. Better schools and colleges were built. Roads and railroads were built. Farmers began growing more tobacco and cotton. Then came the worst war in United States history.

The Northern and Southern states had been arguing for many years. In the South, black people were used as slaves on large farms, called *plantations*. Most people believed that President Lincoln would ban slavery. Southerners' spoke of *states' rights*. They felt that each state should be able to decide for itself about slavery, taxes known as *tariffs*, and other issues. Southern states began to *secede*, or leave the United States. They formed their own country—the Confederate (kun • FED • uh • rut) States of America.

The Civil War began on April 12, 1861. Early that morning, Southern (Confederate) troops fired on Northern (Union) troops at Fort Sumter. This was in Charleston, South Carolina.

Only a few North Carolina people owned slaves. But North Carolina was a Southern state. North Carolina seceded from the United States on May 20, 1861. North Carolina sent more than 140,000 men to fight in the Confederate army. At least ten Civil War battles were fought in North Carolina. The biggest was won by the Union at Bentonville. This bloody battle was fought between March 19 and 21, 1865. By the time the guns were quiet, more than 2,600 Confederate men and 1,600 Union men lay dead or wounded.

Two months later, the last Confederate troops surrendered. The South had lost the Civil War. No state had suffered more than North Carolina. North Carolina lost more men—over 40,000—than any other Confederate state.

Much of the state lay in ruin. Schools, factories, roads, and bridges were destroyed. Farms were growing up in weeds. Men who went home to their farms even found it hard to get seeds for crops.

After the Civil War, a North Carolina man, Andrew Johnson, became president. North Carolina once again became part of the United States.

The United States government began *Reconstruction* (ree • kun • STRUK • shun). This was meant to help rebuild the South. What happened was that Northerners went down to North Carolina. They took over the government. They carried everything they owned with them in carpet bags. They were called *carpetbaggers*. The people of North Carolina started working to rebuild their own state.

A Bicentennial reeanactment of the Civil War years

Left: One of the Wright
    gliders that led to the
    Wright powered airplane
Above: Wilbur Wright
Right: Orville Wright

In 1903 North Carolina was the scene of one of the most famous events in world history. Orville and Wilbur Wright had built an airplane. They lived in Ohio. The Weather Bureau told them the best place to try flying was near Kitty Hawk, North Carolina. On December 17, 1903 the Wright Brothers prepared their flying machine at Kill Devil Hill. This is a big sand dune near Kitty Hawk. Orville piloted the plane first. The airplane took off. It flew 120 feet. This was the first airplane flight. In a later flight that day, Wilbur flew 852 feet.

North Carolina grew fast in the early 1900s. Farmers grew tobacco in North Carolina. Big tobacco factories were built. They turned the tobacco into cigarettes and cigars. By 1930 North Carolina was the leading tobacco state. It still is today.

North Carolina had a lot of trees. North Carolinians realized that trees were like "green gold." They cut down trees. The wood was sent to factories. There it was made into furniture. North Carolina became the leading furniture-making state. It still is today.

Many clothes you wear are made of cotton. There were a lot of cotton fields in North Carolina. North Carolinians set up textile mills. There the cotton was spun into cloth for clothes. North Carolina became the leading textile (cloth-making) state—and it still is today!

Bell Tower, University
of North Carolina

Throughout the 1900s more and more people left their farms. They moved to big cities like Charlotte, Greensboro, Raleigh, and Winston-Salem. In these cities many people work in factories. They make tobacco products, furniture, and cloth.

Today North Carolina factories buzz night and day. Now the state never sleeps!

Today, the state also has fine colleges and universities. Three of these are Duke, North Carolina State University, and the University of North Carolina.

You have learned about some of North Carolina's history. Now it is time for a trip—in words and pictures—through the Tar Heel State.

From the air, you'll get a good view of North Carolina. In the west, the green Appalachian Mountains seem to reach up to your airplane. The western part of the state is sometimes called the *Mountain Region.*

Most of the state's big cities are in the middle of the state. This hilly area is known as the *Piedmont Plateau* (PEED • mahnt platt • TOE).

The eastern part of the state is known as the *Atlantic Coastal Plain.* It is flat land near the ocean. The Coastal Plain has the best farmland in the state.

Cape Hatteras National Seashore on the Atlantic Coastal Plain

The U.S.S. *North Carolina* in her berth on the Cape Fear River

Your airplane is landing in southeastern North Carolina. You have arrived in the city of Wilmington. It is a good place to begin your trip through the state.

In days of old, pirates chased ships near Wilmington. During the Civil War, supplies for the Confederate army were sent to Wilmington.

Today, you can see a very famous ship on the Cape Fear River in Wilmington. It is the U.S.S. *North Carolina*. During World War II, this was the most powerful United States battleship on the Pacific Ocean. It shot down many planes. After the war, the *North Carolina* was about to go to the junk dealer. But the people of North Carolina wouldn't let that happen. They

Beaufort waterfront scene

paid to have it brought to Wilmington. You can walk onto this huge battleship.

Travel up the North Carolina coast from Wilmington. You will see how the ocean has been so important to the state. Beaufort looks much as it did 150 years ago. Whaling ships left the port back then. Blackbeard sailed his ship, the *Queen Anne's Revenge,* around Beaufort Harbor. Nearby Morehead City is a big fishing city. Boats from there go out onto the ocean to catch fish. Menhaden (men • HAYD • un), crabs, shrimps, marlin, and mackerel (MACK • er • ull) are just some kinds of seafood caught in North Carolina waters. North Carolina seafood is sent to many places in America.

29

You can take a boat to Ocracoke Island. It is about 20 miles off the shore. Once, this was the hiding place of Blackbeard.

At times, Blackbeard didn't even have to stop a ship to rob it. Many ships were wrecked on the North Carolina coast. Cape Hatteras—near Ocracoke Island—became known as the "Graveyard of the Atlantic." All Blackbeard had to do was board a wrecked ship and steal the booty!

Below: Ocracoke Island today
Right: Black skimmers at dusk, Ocracoke

These four ships are among the many that have been wrecked at Cape Hatteras, the "Graveyard of the Atlantic."

Today, lighthouses guide ships safely to shore. The Cape Hatteras Lighthouse was built in 1870. It is the tallest brick lighthouse in the United States.

Farther north up the Carolina coast visit Fort Raleigh National Historic Site. It was here that the first English colony in America was founded, in 1585. It was here also that Virginia Dare and the "Lost Colony" vanished.

Southwest of Fort Raleigh is Bath. It is North Carolina's oldest town. It was founded in 1706. Farther inland is New Bern. There, visit rebuilt Tryon Palace. It was the huge home of William Tryon, the English governor of North Carolina. The palace also served as the capitol building when North Carolina was an English colony.

As you travel farther west in the Coastal Plain, you will pass corn fields. You will pass sweet potato fields. You will pass fields of soybeans and peanuts. But the crop you will see the most is tobacco. Tobacco needs a

Tyron Palace restoration, New Bern

warm climate. North Carolina is perfect. The tobacco seeds are planted in late winter. The tobacco plants take about three months to grow. Then machines cut off the leaves. Tobacco leaves are dried. Then they are sent to big-city factories. There they are made into cigarettes and cigars.

Fayetteville (FAY • et • vill) is on the Cape Fear River. It is in the southcentral part of the state. Much tobacco is bought and sold in this city. Visit Market House. At this same place once stood a building that burned down. It was the Convention Hall. There North Carolina approved the United States Constitution in 1789. Fort Bragg is near Fayetteville. Airborne units of the United States Army are trained there.

North Carolina's biggest cities are in the area known as the Piedmont Plateau in the middle of the state.

Raleigh, Durham (DOO • rum), Greensboro, High Point, Winston-Salem, and Charlotte are six big cities in this area.

The
state capitol,
Raleigh

Raleigh is the capital of North Carolina. Visit the
state capitol building. Visit the legislative building.
There you can watch lawmakers working for the Tar
Heel State.

When North Carolina became a state, many towns
wanted to become the capital. New Bern was the capital
from 1766 to 1792. In 1792 North Carolina lawmakers
built a *new* town for their capital. They named it after
Sir Walter Raleigh.

Today, Raleigh is the third biggest city in the state. It
is a good place to exercise your brain. At the North
Carolina Museum of Art you can see some of the world's

famous paintings. At the Museum of Natural History you can learn about dinosaurs and early North Carolina people.

Visit the Andrew Johnson Birthplace, in Raleigh. Our seventeeth president was born in this tiny house, on December 29, 1808.

Durham is about 25 miles northwest of Raleigh. There you can visit a cigarette factory. You will see how tobacco is made into cigarettes.

Durham was named after Dr. Bartlett Durham, who helped found the town about 1853.

After the Civil War, a soldier named Washington Duke started a tobacco company. It grew into one of the biggest in America. His son, James Buchanan (byoo • CAN • an) Duke, gave money to help build Duke University.

Another great school is the University of North Carolina. It is in nearby Chapel Hill. It is the oldest state university in America. Its first building is still in use.

Greensboro is about 55 miles west of Durham. Greensboro was founded in about 1808. The city was named after General Nathanael Greene. He led the American soldiers at Guilford Courthouse.

High Point is just 17 miles southwest of Greensboro. It is sometimes called the "furniture capital of the world."

Winston-Salem is just northwest of High Point. It is the fourth biggest city in the state. A religious group, the Moravians (more • RAVE • ee • unz), formed Salem in 1766. Winston was founded almost a hundred years later. They joined to become one city—Winston-Salem—in 1913.

Winston-Salem skyline

Above: Reynolds House in Winston-Salem, the former
home of tobacco millionaire R.J. Reynolds.
Left: Costumed tour guides at Old Salem

Winston-Salem is a cigarette-making city. Telephones, beer, and underwear are also made in the city.

Visit Old Salem. It has been restored and rebuilt. It now looks as it did over 200 years ago. On Easter, you can see the Moravian Easter Service at sunrise.

About 75 miles southwest of Winston-Salem is the state's biggest city. This is Charlotte. Catawba Indians once lived in the area. Settlers arrived about 1748. The Hezekiah Alexander (hez • ih • KYE • ah al • ex • AND • er) Homesite here was built in 1774. It is the oldest house standing in the city. Charlotte was named after Queen Charlotte, wife of an English king. This pretty city is still called the "Queen City."

In May the World 600 Stock Car Race is held at the Charlotte Motor Speedway. This is one of the richest and longest car races. Other car and motorcycle races are held at the Speedway throughout the year.

There are people of all colors and ethnic groups in Charlotte. There are many black people. In the state, more than one of every five persons is of Afro-American heritage.

You have visited the cities of the Piedmont Plateau. Now head west into the Appalachian Mountains. You'll see tall mountains, sparkling waterfalls, and deep caves. This area is called "The Land of the Sky."

Get on your hiking shoes and visit Grandfather Mountain, near Linville. You can see that Grandfather Mountain looks much like the face of an old man. You can walk across the face of Grandfather Mountain. A mile-high swinging bridge connects two peaks.

Blowing Rock is near Grandfather Mountain. You may think that when you drop something it falls down. But when you throw something off Blowing Rock it often blows right back up to you. That is because of the wind currents there.

About 40 miles southwest of Grandfather Mountain is Mount Mitchell. It is 6,684 feet high. That makes it the tallest peak east of the Mississippi River.

Chimney Rock is about 25 miles south of Mount Mitchell. It is shaped like a giant chimney. It towers 225 feet into the sky. Take an elevator to the top. You will have a breathtaking view of the surrounding mountains. You can see land that trailblazer Daniel Boone explored when he lived in North Carolina.

Mount Mitchell

Scenic
Pilot Mountain

Many people live in the mountains of North Carolina. Some live in log cabins built 200 years ago. Mountain towns might have a thousand people or less. The town names are interesting: Bat Cave, Plumtree, Horse Shoe, Deep Gap, Shooting Creek, Sunshine, Crabtree . . .

Some mountain people have left their homes to find work in cities such as Asheville. Asheville is the biggest city in the western part of the state. Many handicrafts made by mountain people are sold in Asheville stores. Clothes and wood products are also made in Asheville.

You can visit the Biltmore Estate in Asheville. It is said that George Vanderbilt wanted to build the biggest house in the most beautiful place on earth.

The Cherokee Indians are one of America's great tribes. More than a hundred years ago they had books and newspapers written in their own language. When the Cherokee were removed on the Trail of Tears, some hid in the North Carolina mountains. The Indians still have a home there. In the far western part of the state is the Cherokee Indian Reservation. It is at the town of Cherokee.

You can see the play "Unto These Hills" during the summer. It tells the story of the Cherokee. At the Oconaluftee (oh • kah • nah • LUFF • tee) Village on the reservation you can see what Cherokee houses and life were like 250 years ago.

Nearby is the Great Smoky Mountains National Park. People like to hike, camp, and fish in this wild area. There are tall mountains and lovely wild flowers.

White freshwater pond lily at Buxton Museum of the Sea

People aren't the only ones who like the Great Smokies. Many black bear and deer live in North Carolina. There are also foxes, minks, skunks, otters, and beavers in this lovely state.

Home to Cherokee Indians . . . Virginia Dare . . . and presidents.

Land where the people of the "Lost Colony" lived . . . where Blackbeard and other pirates lurked . . . where the Wright Brothers first flew their airplane.

A beautiful state of mountains . . . seashore . . . wild flowers . . . and wild animals.

The leading furniture-making . . . tobacco-growing . . . and textile state.

This is the Tar Heel State—North Carolina.

Facts About NORTH CAROLINA

Area—52,586 square miles (28th biggest state)

Borders—Virginia on the north; the Atlantic Ocean on the east; South Carolina and Georgia on the south; Tennessee on the west

Highest Point—6,684 feet above sea level (Mount Mitchell)

Lowest Point—Sea level (along the Atlantic shore)

Hottest Recorded Temperature—109° F. (at Albemarle on July 28, 1940, and also in Weldon on September 7, 1954)

Coldest Recorded Temperature—Minus 29° F. (at the state's highest point, Mount Mitchell, on January 30, 1966)

Statehood—November 21, 1789, our 12th state and one of the original thirteen

Capital—Raleigh

Previous Capital—New Bern

U. S. Senators—2

U. S. Representatives—11

Counties—100

State Senators—50

State Representatives—120

Origin of Name North Carolina—To honor King Charles I of England; name kept to honor King Charles II of England.

Nickname—Tar Heel State

State Motto—*Esse quam videri* (Latin for "To be, rather than to seem")

State Flower—Flowering Dogwood

State Tree—Pine

State Bird—Cardinal

State Mammal—Gray squirrel

State Insect—Honey bee

State Gem Stone—Emerald

State Shell—Scotch bonnet

State Colors—Red and blue

State Flag—Adopted in 1885

State Seal—Adopted in 1971

State Song—"The Old North State" by William Gaston and Mrs. E. E. Randolph

Some Rivers—Roanoke, Tar, Neuse, Cape Fear, Pee Dee, French Broad, Chowan, Yadkin, Catawba

Some Waterfalls—Bridal Veil Falls, Linville Falls, Whitewater Falls, Looking Glass Falls

Some Ranges of the Appalachian Mountains—Great Smoky, Bald, Black, Brushy, Iron, South, Stone, Unaka

Wildlife—Black bear, deer, foxes, beaver, gray squirrels, rabbits, opossums, otters, skunks, raccoons, muskrats, wildcats, many kinds of birds and fish

Fishing—Crabs, menhaden, oysters, shrimp, marlin, mackerel

Farm products—Tobacco, soybeans, corn, hogs, sweet potatoes, peanuts,
   cotton, milk and other dairy products, poultry, beef cattle
Manufacturing Products—Textiles (cloth products), hosiery, tobacco
   products, chemicals, machinery, food products, furniture and other wood
   products, lumber, computers, clothes, metal products, plastic products,
   rubber products, glass products, paper
Mining—Stone, feldspar, granite, tungsten, mica, clay, talc, sand, gravel
Population—5,881,813 (1980 census)
Population Density—112 people per square mile
Population Distribution—52 percent rural (farm areas)
                        48 percent urban (city areas)
Biggest Cities—Charlotte 314,447
               Greensboro 155,642
               Raleigh 150,255
               Winston-Salem 131,885
               Durham 100,538

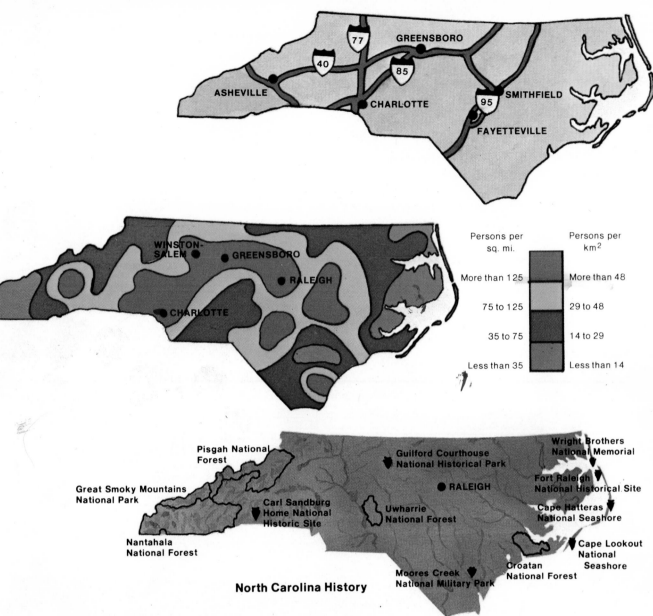

North Carolina History

Persons per sq. mi. | Persons per km²
More than 125 | More than 48
75 to 125 | 29 to 48
35 to 75 | 14 to 29
Less than 35 | Less than 14

People lived in North Carolina at least 10,000 years ago.

1524—Giovanni da Verrazano explores the coast of North Carolina

1526—About this time, Spaniard Lucas Vásquez de Ayllón establishes a colony near Cape Fear that lasts a short time

1540—Hernando De Soto, looking for gold, explores western mountains of North Carolina

1584—English explorers under Captains Arthur Barlowe and Philip Amadas are sent by Sir Walter Raleigh

1585—First English colony in what is now the United States is established at Roanoke Island

1587—Second colony is established, with John White as leader; Virginia Dare is born there

45

1590—When John White returns, "Lost Colony" has vanished

1629—King Charles I of England grants *Carolana* to Robert Heath

1650—Settlers from Virginia begin arriving

1663—King Charles II of England grants Carolina colony to eight noblemen known as Lords Proprietors

1706—First town—Bath—founded

1711—Beginning of Tuscarora War between Indians and settlers

1712—North Carolina and South Carolina become separate colonies

1713—Indians defeated as Tuscarora War ends on March 25

1729—North Carolina becomes a royal colony

1767—Andrew Jackson, 7th president of the United States, is born in the Waxhaw settlement along the unsurveyed North Carolina-South Carolina border on March 15

1768—Charlotte is founded and grows into North Carolina's biggest city by the twentieth century

1774—North Carolina sends delegates to First Continental Congress

1775—Revolutionary War begins on April 19

1776—North Carolina is first colony to vote for independence

1783—Revolutionary War ends; United States of America has been born!

1789—North Carolina becomes our 12th state on November 21

1792—Capital of state, Raleigh, is founded

1795—University of North Carolina, founded in 1789, opens

1795—James K. Polk, 11th President of United States, is born near Pineville on November 2

1808—Andrew Johnson, 17th President of United States, is born in Raleigh on December 29

1820—Population of Tar Heel State is 638,829

1861—Civil War begins on April 12; North Carolina secedes from United States on May 20

1865—Confederate General Joseph E. Johnston surrenders his forces to Union General William T. Sherman, near Durham; Civil War ends and Reconstruction begins

1868—North Carolina is readmitted to the United States

1903—Wright Brothers make first successful airplane flight near Kitty Hawk

1914-1918—During World War I, over 86,000 Tar Heels fight

1930—By now, North Carolina is number one state in producing cotton textiles, tobacco products, and wooden furniture

1939-1945—During World War II, over 362,000 Tar Heels fight

1945—Fontana Dam, biggest dam in North Carolina, is built

1957—Duke University, University of North Carolina, and North Carolina State University establish Research Triangle

1971—Present state constitution goes into effect

1979—Fourteen Ku Klux Klansmen arraigned on murder charges after five demonstrators, preparing for anti-Klan march, are shot in Greensboro

1984—A battery of tornadoes cut path 260 miles long through both North and South Carolina, injuring over 1,000 and killing over 61 people

INDEX

INDEX, Cont'd.

About the Author:

Dennis Fradin attended Northwestern University on a creative writing scholarship and graduated in 1967. While still at Northwestern, he published his first stories in *Ingenue* magazine and also won a prize in *Seventeen's* short story competition. A prolific writer, Dennis Fradin has been regularly publishing stories in such diverse places as *The Saturday Evening Post, Scholastic, National Humane Review, Midwest,* and *The Teaching Paper.* He has also scripted several educational films. Since 1970 he has taught second grade reading in a Chicago school—a rewarding job, which, the author says, "provides a captive audience on whom I test my children's stories." Married and the father of three children, Dennis Fradin spends his free time with his family or playing a myriad of sports and games with his childhood chums.

About the Artists:

Len Meents studied painting and drawing at Southern Illinois University and after graduation in 1969 he moved to Chicago. Mr. Meents works full time as a painter and illustrator. He and his wife and child currently make their home in LaGrange, Illinois.

Richard Wahl, graduate of the Art Center College of Design in Los Angeles, has illustrated a number of magazine articles and booklets. He is a skilled artist and photographer who advocates realistic interpretations of his subjects. He lives with his wife and two sons in Libertyville, Illinois.